I0559742

# HOW TO USE THIS WORKBOOK

Welcome to the Beyond The Mirror Workbook.

In these pages, you'll get to know yourself better, learn about  body image, self-compassion and important tools that can help you treat yourself with the kindness and respect you truly deserve. (For more on self-compassion, check out Kristen Neff's amazing original research on the topic.)

Learning to care for yourself in new ways takes practice. But it's so worth it!

I hope these exercises help you as much as they've helped me… and the girls in the Mirror Diary Series! Make sure you check out book one of The Mirror Diaries , Finding Grace, to see how she navigates these challenges.

XO,
Vanessa Coulbeck

Want to learn more or get a PDF version of this workbook to print? Visit **StrongGirlPublishing.com/beyond-the-mirror** to  access more printable worksheets, pump-up playlists + more!

# what is self-compassion?

Self-compassion means being kind to yourself, just like you would be to a close friend. Self-compassion isn't about fixing all your problems at once. It's about being kind to yourself, especially when you're struggling.

**There are 3 parts to practicing self-compassion:**
1. Mindfulness, which means noticing what we're feeling without getting overwhelmed by it
2. Self-kindness, which is speaking to ourselves with gentle words, just like how we would talk to a friend, and finally,
3. Common humanity, which sounds complicated but just means remembering that everyone makes mistakes, and nobody is perfect. We're all in this together.

**Self-compassion is actually really good for us:**
• It helps improve body image and body appreciation (even when our bodies are changing).
• It lowers anxiety and makes us better able to handle things like stress and rejection.
• It helps us eat more intuitively, which means paying attention to how food makes us feel, not how it looks.
• It leads to healthier friendships (because we're not constantly comparing ourselves).
• It helps us cope better with tough stuff, like getting our periods, switching schools, or drama with friends.
• And most of all, it teaches us we are worthy, even when we mess up, feel awkward, or don't "fit in."

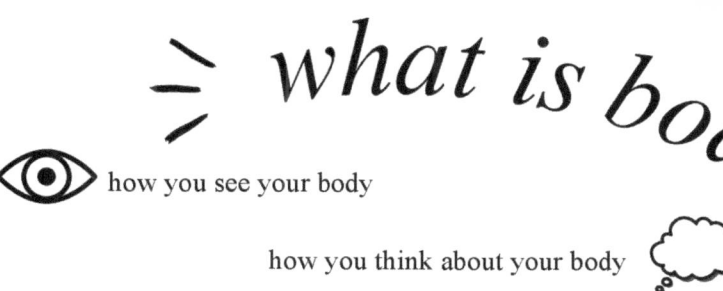

# what is body image?

how you see your body

how you think about your body

how you feel about your body

your behaviors towards your body

Body image is how you think and feel about your body. It can be positive, negative, or a mix of both—and it can change depending on the day, the situation, or even your mood. Your body image is shaped by things inside you, like your personality, and things outside you, like your friends, family, and social media.

Having a positive body image means you can accept, appreciate, and respect your body, even if there are things you wish were different. You can feel dissatisfied with parts of your body but still value and care for it. Positive body image is important because it helps protect you from things like unhealthy habits or negative self-talk.

**Benefits of a positive body image**

- Higher self-esteem: Feeling good about yourself can make life happier and make you more confident.
- Self-acceptance: Being comfortable in your body makes it easier to ignore unrealistic beauty standards in media and society.
- Healthy habits: When you listen to your body and respect it, it's easier to make choices that are good for your health, like moving, eating, and resting in ways that feel right for you.
- Better mental health: Positive body image is linked to lower stress, anxiety, and depression.
- Stronger relationships: When you feel good about yourself, it can be easier to connect with others and build supportive friendships.
- Resilience: Feeling comfortable in your body helps you cope better with challenges and setbacks.
- Greater confidence in trying new things: Believing in yourself and your body can make it easier to explore activities, sports, or experiences without fear.

*Sometimes we think about how our body looks,*
*but how often do we think about what our body can do?*

# *Future Me letter*

Write a letter to Future You—you at this time next year, or maybe even you in five or ten years!—and include what you're excited for, what kind of person you want to be by the time you're reading this letter in the future, and anything you're nervous about now. Bonus points if you take a photo of this when you're done and schedule it as an email that will send  to Future You!

# *AFFIRMATION CREATION*

Add your favourite affirmations or use the ones provided.
Print, cut and choose a random card every day!

I AM ENOUGH,
JUST AS I AM.

I CAN BE GENTLE
WITH MYSELF.

MY BODY IS STRONG
AND CAPABLE.

I AM PROUD OF
EVERYTHING MY BODY
DOES FOR ME.

# *Treat* Yourself *as You Would a* Friend

Imagine one of your best friends is having a really hard time or feeling super bad about themselves. How would you help them? What would you say to make them feel better?
What would you do for them? How would your voice sound when you're talking to them?

---------------------------------------------------------------------------------------------------

---------------------------------------------------------------------------------------------------

---------------------------------------------------------------------------------------------------

Now think about a time when *you* were feeling upset or struggling. How did you talk to yourself? What did you say to yourself? What did you do? What tone of voice did you use in your head?

---------------------------------------------------------------------------------------------------

---------------------------------------------------------------------------------------------------

---------------------------------------------------------------------------------------------------

Look at your answers. Are they different? _____ Yes        _____ No

If they are different, why do you think you treat yourself differently than you treat your friends? What things make it harder to be kind to yourself?

---------------------------------------------------------------------------------------------------

---------------------------------------------------------------------------------------------------

---------------------------------------------------------------------------------------------------

Imagine if you spoke to yourself the same way you'd speak to a friend when they're feeling down. How do you think that would feel? How might it help you?

---------------------------------------------------------------------------------------------------

---------------------------------------------------------------------------------------------------

---------------------------------------------------------------------------------------------------

**Try it the next time you're feeling upset: Treat yourself like your own best friend and see what happens!**

# Create a Body Appreciation Map

Body appreciation goes beyond what you see in the mirror, but sometimes it can be hard to put these feelings into words or images. Here, your goal is to think about what you appreciate about each body part based on what it helps you do—not how it looks.

**Here are a few examples to get you started:**

| Body Part | What It Helps Me Do | Why That Matters to Me |
|---|---|---|
| Arms & Hands | Write, create art, hug a friend | I love painting and expressing myself. Giving hugs makes me feel close to people I care about. |
| Legs & Feet | Run, dance, explore, play sports | My legs help me play soccer, which brings me joy and helps me feel strong and free. |
| Heart & Lungs | Keep me alive, help me breathe, give me energy | They help me keep up with my friends and feel energized when I'm outside playing. |
| Eyes & Ears | Read books, watch movies, listen to music | I love reading and music. They help me feel calm and happy. |
| Skin & Touch | Feel textures, hugs, warmth, comfort | When I snuggle with my dog or wrap up in a cozy blanket, I feel safe and loved. |
| Voice & Mouth | Talk, laugh, sing, eat | I love singing and talking to my friends. It helps me feel connected. |

# My *Body Appreciation* Map

Draw yourself in any way you like, label parts of your body, and think about what you appreciate about each part based on what it helps you do.

This exercise helps us focus on what our bodies do for us, not just how they look. It's a way to be kind and thankful to ourselves for all the amazing things our bodies help us with every day!

**Draw Yourself:** It doesn't have to be fancy, stick figures are totally allowed! (You can also cut out a photo and put it there instead!

**Label Your Body Parts**: After you draw yourself, label the different parts of your body. You can choose to label parts like your head, arms, legs, hands, feet, heart, eyes, hair, stomach, and more. It's up to you! Use arrows or lines to point to each part of your body.

**Think About What Each Part Does:** Now, look at each part you labeled and think about what it helps you do. For example, your arms help you hug, your legs help you run, your stomach helps you digest food, etc.

**Get Appreciative.** Write down what you appreciate about each body part and how it helps you in your everyday life. You can use the following prompts to help you:
"I appreciate my ___ because it helps me ___."
"My ___ helps me ___ and I'm thankful for that because ___."

Here are some examples to help you get started:
- Legs: "I appreciate my legs because they help me run fast and jump high, especially when I play sports!"
- Arms: "I appreciate my arms because they help me hug my friends and lift things I need."
- Eyes: "I appreciate my eyes because they help me see my favorite things, like books."
- Hands: "I appreciate my hands because they help me draw and write, and give high fives!"

**Review and Reflect:** Once you've filled in the chart for each body part, take a moment to look at everything you've written. Think about how all your body parts work together to help you do amazing things every day.

# *Box Breathing* 101

Mindfulness is about paying attention to the present moment instead of getting stuck in the past or worrying about the future. It helps you notice your thoughts and feelings without judging them. A great way to practice mindfulness is through box breathing, which can help you feel calmer and more focused.

Steps:
1. Sit comfortably in a quiet place with your back straight.
2. Breathe in through your nose for a count of 4. (Imagine filling your lungs with air as if you're drawing air up into your chest.)
3. Hold your breath for a count of 4. (Keep your chest full without feeling tense.)
4. Breathe out through your mouth for a count of 4. (Release all the air slowly and fully.)
5. Hold your breath again for a count of 4 before starting the next round.
6. Repeat this cycle for 4-5 rounds, focusing on the rhythm of your breath.

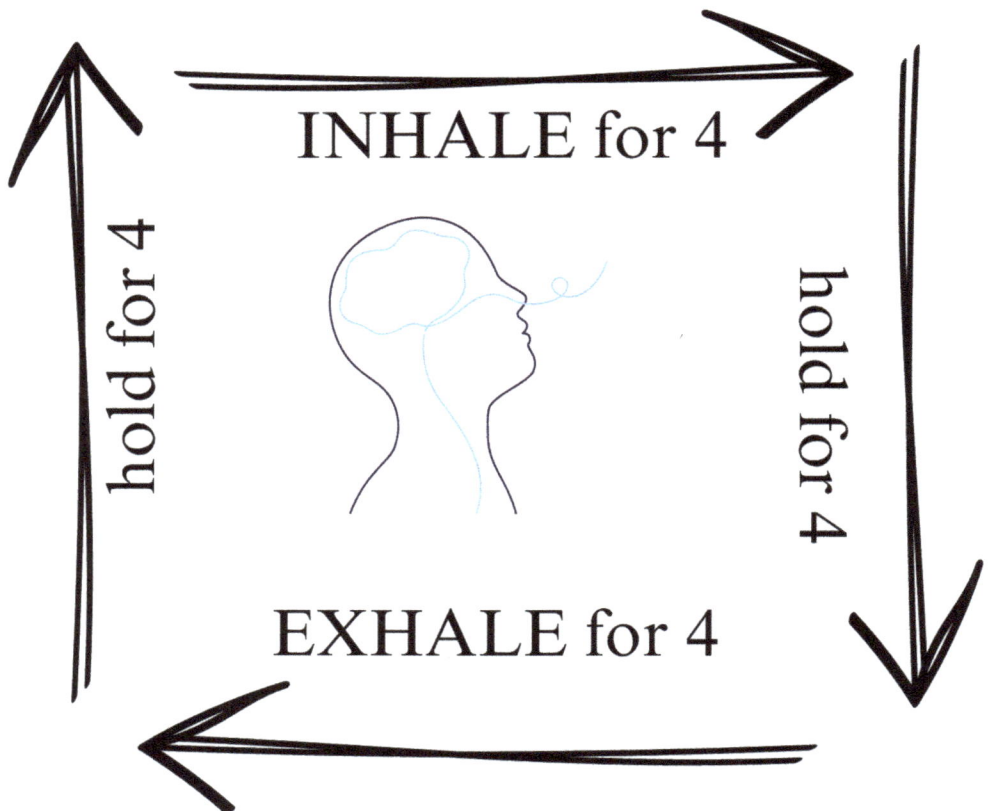

# THERE IS MAGIC IN HOW YOU KEEP GOING, EVEN WHEN IT'S HARD.

# *Beyond The Mirror* Exercise

*The Beyond the Mirror Exercise helps us build a positive relationship with our reflection. It reminds us to be kind to ourselves, which helps grow self-compassion and encourages us to see ourselves in a more positive light.*

**Stand in Front of the Mirror:** Find a mirror and stand in front of it. Take a moment to look at yourself. Think of your reflection as a friend, instead of seeing a mirror as something that makes you feel judgmental and be critical, see it as a space where you can say kind things to yourself. Take a moment to think about who you are beyond how you look.

**Complete these two statements:**

I am...                               I can...

**Examples:**

I am thoughtful and always try to help others.

I am strong, and I don't give up when things get hard.

I can do hard things, even when I feel nervous.

I can be confident in who I am and not compare myself to others.

**Try it here!**

I am _____

I can _____

I am _____

I can _____

I am _____

I can _____

**See the Power in Yourself**

 Take a deep breath and look at yourself recognizing your strength and uniqueness.

Test out the affirmations you just wrote out loud while looking at yourself.

You can also try out a few of these to find one to three affirmations that feel right for you"

- "I am worthy of love and kindness."
- "I can face challenges and keep going."
- "I am strong, inside and out."
- "I can be proud of myself for trying new things."

**Notice how you feel after saying these affirmations. Does it feel different than what you usually tell yourself?**

**After completing the exercise, take a moment to reflect:**
- How did saying these affirmations make you feel?
- Which affirmation felt the most powerful?
- How can you remind yourself of these affirmations daily?

**Write out your favorite affirmations and stick them on the mirror in your room or bathroom so you can be reminded of them regularly!**

SOME DAYS YOU'LL BLOOM, SOME DAYS YOU'LL REST. BOTH ARE BEAUTIFUL.

# *self-compassion*
# Emotion *Tracker*

Use this exercise anytime you're feeling a strong emotion (good or bad!). It's a great way to get in touch with your emotions and better understand them.

---

*( Day ):*           *( Month ):*           *( Year ):*

---

### *How Are You Feeling Right Now?*
*(hoose the emotion(s) that best describe how you feel. You can circle or write your own.*

- 😊 HAPPY
- 😰 ANXIOUS
- 😡 ANGRY
- 😢 SAD
- 😃 EXCITED
- 😤 FRUSTRATED
- 😳 EMBARRASSED
- 😟 WORRIED
- 😎 CONFIDENT
- 😯 SURPRISED
- 😕 CONFUSED
- 😴 TIRED
- 😍 PROUD
- ✨ GRATEFUL
- _____ OTHER

*How Strong Is the Emotion on a scale of 1 to 10?* _____

### *What Happened to Make You Feel This Way?*
*Think about what triggered this emotion. Was it a person, a situation, or something you thought about?*

### *How Did Your Body Feel?*
*How did your body react when you felt this emotion? Did your heart race, did you feel tense, or did you feel calm?*

---

**Kindness to Yourself Practice:** Take a deep breath. It's okay to feel this way. Write something kind to yourself about this emotion, like you would tell a friend who feels the same way. (Example: "It's okay to feel upset," or "I'm proud of myself for noticing how I feel.")

**What Could You Do to Be Kind to Yourself Right Now?** What is one thing you can do to help yourself feel better or comfort yourself? It could be something small like taking deep breaths, talking to someone you trust, or doing something fun.

**Self-Compassion Practice:** Write or draw something that helps you feel better or shows self-compassion. It could be a quote, an affirmation, or something you like doing to feel calm. You can also practice deep breathing or self-soothing activities.

**How Would You Like to Feel?** Think about how you would like to feel now. You can keep the same emotion or choose a new one. What would help you feel more peaceful or happy?

**Reflection**: At the end of the week, look back at your logs. How have you been kind to yourself? How did that help you with your feelings? Did you notice anything new about how you react to certain emotions?

# *What aspects of* self-compassion *do you need right now?*

Self-compassion is more than just being kind to yourself—it has different aspects that help us feel safe, supported, and motivated. Below are six ways you can practice self-compassion. Read through them and think about which one you might need most right now:

**Comforting** – Supporting yourself like you would a friend when you're feeling down.
*Example: "I am gentle with myself when I make mistakes."*

**Soothing** – Helping yourself feel calm and relaxed, especially when things feel stressful.
*Example: "I can take deep breaths and remind myself that I am okay."*

**Validating** – Recognizing and accepting your own feelings as real and important.
*Example: "I am allowed to feel what I feel, and my emotions matter."*

**Protecting** – Setting boundaries and standing up for yourself when needed.
*Example: "I can say no to things that make me uncomfortable or unsafe."*

**Providing** – Giving yourself what you truly need, whether it's rest, support, or fun.
*Example: "I can take breaks when I need them, and that's okay."*

**Motivating** – Encouraging yourself like a good coach—with kindness instead of criticism.
*Example: "I am capable, and I can keep going even when things feel hard."*

Take a moment to think about how you treat yourself. Self-compassion means being kind to yourself, just like you would be to a close friend. Read the questions below and reflect on what you might need most right now:

**Comfort: Do you ever feel frustrated with yourself when trying something new or difficult? Would it help to remind yourself that mistakes are part of learning and to be gentler with yourself?**

-----------------------------------------------------------------------------------------

-----------------------------------------------------------------------------------------

-----------------------------------------------------------------------------------------

-----------------------------------------------------------------------------------------

**Feeling Safe & Valued: Do you sometimes feel alone in your feelings? Would it help to remind yourself that your emotions are real and that it's okay to feel what you feel?**

-----------------------------------------------------------------------------------------

-----------------------------------------------------------------------------------------

-----------------------------------------------------------------------------------------

-----------------------------------------------------------------------------------------

**Taking Care of Your Needs: Do you listen to what your body and mind need? Would you like to get better at knowing when to rest, take breaks, or ask for help?**

-----------------------------------------------------------------------------------------

-----------------------------------------------------------------------------------------

-----------------------------------------------------------------------------------------

-----------------------------------------------------------------------------------------

**Encouraging Yourself: When things get hard, do you motivate yourself with kindness or criticism? Would it help to talk to yourself like a supportive coach instead of being too hard on yourself?**

-----------------------------------------------------------------------------------------

-----------------------------------------------------------------------------------------

-----------------------------------------------------------------------------------------

# EVERY DAY IS A NEW PAGE. YOU GET TO DECIDE WHAT YOU'LL WRITE.

# Create a *Power Up* Morning Routine

**It only takes a few minutes to start your day on the right foot. Even making a few minutes for me-time can set a good tone for the day. Can you plan a 5-minute morning routine that feels good for you?**

**Consider adding:**

- Taking a few deep breaths (maybe doing a round of Box Breathing) right when you wake up
- Reading your Mirror Affirmation  while brushing your teeth and washing your face
- Have a mini-dance party to a favorite song (get our fave playlist at StrongGirlPublishing.com/mirror)
- Get dressed, eat breakfast, head to school!

Make your morning routine plan here:

-------------------------------------------------------------------------------------------------------

-------------------------------------------------------------------------------------------------------

-------------------------------------------------------------------------------------------------------

-------------------------------------------------------------------------------------------------------

-------------------------------------------------------------------------------------------------------

-------------------------------------------------------------------------------------------------------

After a few days, come back and re-assess. Have you been sticking to it? How has it made you feel? If you've struggled to do it, is there a way you can make it easier and try again?

-------------------------------------------------------------------------------------------------------

-------------------------------------------------------------------------------------------------------

-------------------------------------------------------------------------------------------------------

-------------------------------------------------------------------------------------------------------

-------------------------------------------------------------------------------------------------------

# *Self-Compassion* Break

Think about a situation in your life that feels hard or stressful right now. Maybe it's a tough day at school, a disagreement with a friend, or feeling nervous about something. Take a deep breath and notice how this stress feels in your body. **Now, say to yourself:**

**Know: This is a tough moment.**
- That's mindfulness—recognizing what's happening without ignoring it.
- Other ways to say this:
  - "This feels really hard right now."
  - "I don't like how this feels."
  - "This is stress, and that's okay."

**Understand**: **Struggles are part of life.**
- That's realizing that everyone makes mistakes and deals with hard times. It's helpful to remind yourself that you're not alone when you are struggling.
- Other ways to say this:
  - "Everyone has hard days."
  - "I'm not the only one who feels this way."
  - "It's okay to struggle sometimes."

Now, place your hands over your heart or give yourself a gentle hug—whatever feels most comforting. Take another deep breath.

**Ask Yourself: What do I need to hear right now?**
- Choose a phrase that feels right for you:
  - May I give myself the kindness I need.
  - May I accept myself just as I am.
  - May I be patient with myself.
  - May I be strong.
  - May I remember that I am enough.

You can use this anytime you're feeling overwhelmed. Self-compassion isn't about ignoring hard feelings—it's about learning to be there for yourself, just like you would for a friend.

# *Getting Mindful*
# Breathe & Believe *Pocket Card*

Sometimes, we need a little cue to put us in the right state of mind. Use the cards below to create your next steps towards mindfulness.

A Calm Word – Write down your calm word (This will become a mantra you can repeat)

A Kind Action – Draw a small picture or describe the kind action you'll use (hand on heart)

Your Box Breathing Goal – Set a goal to practice mindful breathing ___ times a week to help with _____ (e.g., nerves before a game, stressful moments, etc.)."

Whenever you feel overwhelmed, stressed, or just need a moment to reset, look at these cards for a reminder and try a few rounds of box breathing to reconnect with yourself!

*calm word*

*kind action*

*box breathing goal*

YOUR VOICE
HAS POWER.
YOUR HEART
HAS POWER.
YOUR KINDNESS
HAS POWER

# *The* Social Media *Comparison Trap*

It's important to keep in mind that social media isn't always real life. It's normally a person's highlight reel, sharing only the things that they want everyone to see. But sometimes, that can make us feel like we don't quite measure up, or we're not doing enough, or we start to feel bad that we don't look a certain way. Rather than letting those types of posts get us down, we can simply notice the feeling— and then come back to our real life, and think of what would make our IRL highlight reel!

## *Social Media Reality Check*

**Think of a post that made you feel bad or like you had to "measure up." What was it?**

**What's one real thing about your life that makes you proud or brings you joy—even if it doesn't get posted?**

**Write a positive reminder to yourself about why social media isn't always reality.** (Take a picture of this reminder and save it on your phone so when you're scrolling, if you start to feel bad, you can revisit it!)

**How can you show up on social media in a way that feels real and authentic to you?**

## *Feel-Good Feed Audit*

If you spend a lot of time on social media, your feed can really impact how you feel. While getting off of social media or limiting your time online is one way to help control those feelings, you can also start to feel more positive by following content that makes you feel inspired and proud of who you are… And you can mute or unfollow accounts that don't make you feel as goon..

**What's one kind of post or account that lifts you up?**

**What's something you can do when a post makes you feel left out, not good enough, or stuck in comparison?**

## *Self-Compassion Check*

Remember: The goal should always be to practice self-kindness instead of comparison. **Write one kind reminder you'll tell yourself next time a post messes with your confidence.**
 (Examples: "I'm more than what I post." / "I don't need to look like her to be enough.")

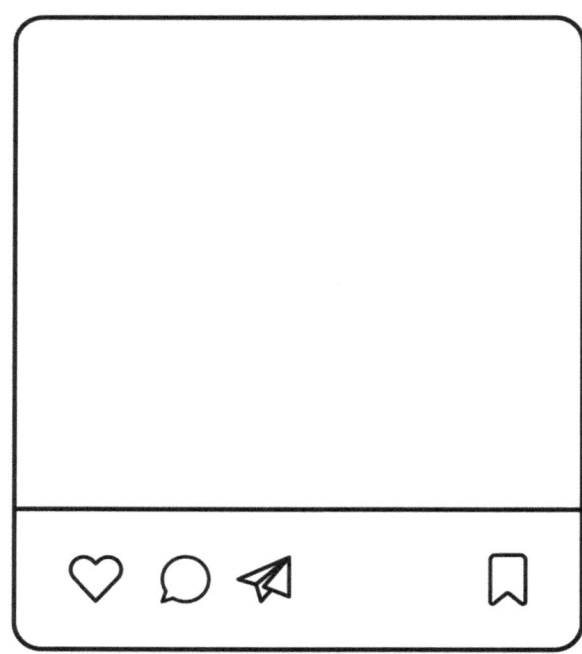

# Check in on Your Affirmations

It's been a while since you first wrote out your affirmations. How are they working for you?
Are there any new ones you want to add, or tweaks to make to the current ones?

# Embrace Authenticity Over Conformity

It can be tempting to follow what everyone else is doing, especially if you feel like you need to fit in. But staying true to who you are—your values, your interests, and what feels right in your heart—is what makes you *really* powerful.

- **You don't have to do something just because everyone else is doing it.** If it doesn't feel right to you, you can make a different choice.
- **Being yourself means standing by what you believe in.** Your opinions, values, and dreams matter, even if they're different from others.
- **Your uniqueness is your strength.** Imagine if superheroes all had the same powers—how boring would that be? The world needs you to be *you!*
- **Remember our affirmation:** *Being myself is my superpower.* You don't have to change to fit in. The people who truly matter will appreciate you for who you are!

**Step 1: What Makes You, You?**

Write down three things that make you unique. These can be your interests, values, or things you care about that may be different from what others think or do.

**Step 2: Stand by Your Values**

Think of a time when you felt pressured to do something because others were doing it, but it didn't feel right to you. How did it make you feel?How would you handle that situation differently now, knowing it's okay to stay true to yourself?

**Step 3: Practice Being Authentic**

Write down one way you can stay true to yourself in the next week, even if it means doing something differently than your friends.

# CELEBRATE THE SMALL VICTORIES. THEY ARE JUST AS IMPORTANT AS THE BIG ONES.

# *Creative Outlet* Exploration

Being yourself means finding ways to show the world who you are—through the things you love, the clothes you wear, or the activities that make you happy. Maybe you love drawing, writing, playing music, or putting together outfits that feel *so you.*

**The more time we spend doing things we love, the happier we feel.** Self-expression is all about showing the world what makes you unique!

## Step 1: Find Your Creative Outlet.

Take a moment to reflect on what makes you, *you!*

- What is something you've always loved doing? *(Examples: painting, writing, playing an instrument, dancing, designing outfits, coding, photography, etc.)*

- What is something you'd like to try but haven't yet?

- If you had a free day to do whatever you wanted, what would you do?

## Step 2: Make Time for YOU

- Your Challenge: Set aside 30 minutes every week to do something creative that makes you feel happy and free! Put it on the calendar so you don't forget.
- Pick one thing from your list, or try something totally new! The only rule is that you release any expectations. This is about creativity and the process, not about creating something "perfect." Next week, you can try something different if you want to!

## Step 3: Reflect on Your Experience

After you've spent time being creative, take a moment to think about how it felt.

**What activity did you choose?**


**How did you feel while doing it? (Circle one or write your own!)**

*Happy*          *Creative*          *Inspired*          *Calm*          *Unique*          *Grateful*

*Other:* _____

**Would you like to do this activity again? Why or why not?**


## Put the Extraordinary into the Ordinary

That was your weekly creative activity, but how can you make it a (shorter) daily practice?
Even the little things you do every day can help you express yourself!
Here are a few simple ways to celebrate who you are:

- Write one sentence about how your day went.
- Sing a song that makes you smile.
- Wear an outfit that feels comfortable and fun to you.

**How will you start to show your creativity on a daily bases?**


Remember: The world is a better place when you show what makes you unique. Your creativity, ideas, and passions are extraordinary! No one is YOU, and that is your superpower.

# Change Your *Frame of Reference*

Sometimes, we notice "flaws" in ourselves that others don't even see—and we talk about ourselves in a way that we would never talk about a friend! Think about how you talk to your best friend, or what you tell other people about them. Write it down!

---------------------------------------------------------------------------------------------------

---------------------------------------------------------------------------------------------------

---------------------------------------------------------------------------------------------------

---------------------------------------------------------------------------------------------------

Now, think about if your best friend described you: What do you think they would say?

---------------------------------------------------------------------------------------------------

---------------------------------------------------------------------------------------------------

---------------------------------------------------------------------------------------------------

How does that compare to how you normally describe yourself in your own head?

---------------------------------------------------------------------------------------------------

---------------------------------------------------------------------------------------------------

---------------------------------------------------------------------------------------------------

What are four kinds thing you can start saying to yourself more often?

-----------------------------------------------------------------------------

-----------------------------------------------------------------------------

-----------------------------------------------------------------------------

-----------------------------------------------------------------------------

# NO ONE ELSE GETS TO DECIDE YOUR STORY — ONLY YOU.

# *Mirror of Me:* My Power Board Collage

Create a body acceptance collage using magazine cutouts, cutouts from the next page, drawings, and words that represent a healthy and confident body image.

 **collage cutouts**

**Be Strong!**

SOCIAL MEDIA FREE®
GO OFFLINE®

**I AM strong**

BREATHE

**YOU GOT THIS**

**ONE DAY AT A TIME**

**GOOD ENERGY**

**AFFIRMATIONS**

GRACE AND GRATITUDE® EVERYDAY®

**GIRL POWER**

**YOU ARE Brave**

YOU ARE HERE

# YOUR DREAMS ARE VALID, NO MATTER HOW BIG OR SMALL THEY SEEM.

# Reflections *on Your Collage*

**Why do you think body acceptance is important?**

------------------------------------------------------------

------------------------------------------------------------

------------------------------------------------------------

------------------------------------------------------------

------------------------------------------------------------

------------------------------------------------------------

------------------------------------------------------------

------------------------------------------------------------

**What did you learn from this activity?**

------------------------------------------------------------

------------------------------------------------------------

------------------------------------------------------------

------------------------------------------------------------

------------------------------------------------------------

------------------------------------------------------------

------------------------------------------------------------

------------------------------------------------------------

**Can you put your collage somewhere—like your closet or in a frame on your desk or bureau—so you'll be reminded of it regularly?**

# *Practice Your* **POWER POSE**

Did you know that how you stand can actually change how you feel? A power pose is a confident, open stance that helps you feel strong, brave, and ready to take on anything. When you stand tall, your brain gets the message that you are powerful!

**Stand up and try one of these poses for 30 seconds to 1 minute:**
- Superhero Pose – Stand with your feet shoulder-width apart, hands on your hips, chin up, and chest lifted.
- Victory Pose – Stand tall, stretch your arms up in a "V" shape, and imagine crossing the finish line of a big race!
- Rockstar Pose – Stand with your legs apart, one hand on your hip, and the other raised like you're about to take the stage.
- Try any other pose that feels confident to you!!

Use Your Power Pose whenever you need a confidence boost—before a big test, a sports game, or speaking in front of a group—try a power pose for one minute. It might feel silly at first, but science shows it can actually help! (Remember: Confidence isn't just about how you feel on the inside—it's also about how you carry yourself on the outside. Stand tall, take up space, and own your power!)

EVEN ON TOUGH
DAYS, YOU ARE
STILL WORTHY
OF KINDNESS...
ESPECIALLY
YOUR OWN.

# *Reflection on* Self-Acceptance

**Self-acceptance is all about recognizing that no one is perfect. We all have our strengths and weaknesses, and that's what makes us unique. Embrace all of it, because it's what makes you— you. It's okay if it's not easy at first; just take it one day at a time. And hey, we're in this together, so let's keep practicing kindness to ourselves!**

### Step 1: Think about your body.

By now, we now what to do here… Take a moment to think about the things your body can do, instead of how it looks. Write down three things you appreciate about your body. They can be small or big, but focus on the things that make your body awesome for what it can do!

---------------------------------------------------------------------------------------------

---------------------------------------------------------------------------------------------

---------------------------------------------------------------------------------------------

---------------------------------------------------------------------------------------------

---------------------------------------------------------------------------------------------

---------------------------------------------------------------------------------------------

### Step 2: Reflect on your activities.

What's one way your body helps you enjoy something you love to do—whether it's a sport, a hobby, or just having fun? It can be anything, as long as it's something that makes you feel good about what your body can do.

---------------------------------------------------------------------------------------------

---------------------------------------------------------------------------------------------

---------------------------------------------------------------------------------------------

---------------------------------------------------------------------------------------------

---------------------------------------------------------------------------------------------

### Step 3: Set an intention.

Think about the next time you start comparing yourself to others. What's one kind or positive thing you'll tell yourself? It could be a reminder that your body is awesome, just as it is, and helps you do the things you love.

Examples:

- *"I don't need to look like anyone else. I'm strong and amazing just as I am!"*
- *"My body helps me do things I enjoy, and that's enough."*
- *"I'm proud of the way I take care of my body."*

Write it here, and write it on a sticky note to put on your mirror as well! (Or you can use a dry erase marker and write directly on your mirror—it will wipe off!)

# Learning to Celebrate Small Wins & Daily High-Fives

Write down a small win at the end of each day—whether it's speaking up in class, tried a new sport, or just got through a tough day. Reflect on how far you've come and celebrate these steps forward—whether it's speaking up in class, trying something new, or just getting through a tough day.

**Try it out: for two weeks, fill in your wins of the day right here!**

# A GRATEFUL HEART IS A HAPPY HEART.

# *Letting Go of Comparison* Exercise

## The Comparison Trap

When we compare ourselves to others, we forget how amazing we already are. Think about a time when you have compared yourself to someone else. Maybe it was about how they looked, how well they did in school or sports, or how popular they seemed. What were you comparing, exactly? How did that make you feel? Write down a few words or draw a small doodle that represents that feeling.

---------------------------------------------------------------------------------

---------------------------------------------------------------------------------

---------------------------------------------------------------------------------

---------------------------------------------------------------------------------

## Reality Check

*Now, take a step back and ask yourself:*

Did this comparison actually help me in any way? (Sometimes the answer might be yes!)

---------------------------------------------------------------------------------

---------------------------------------------------------------------------------

What strengths do I have that make me unique?

---------------------------------------------------------------------------------

---------------------------------------------------------------------------------

If I were my own best friend, what would I say to myself in that moment?

---------------------------------------------------------------------------------

---------------------------------------------------------------------------------

---------------------------------------------------------------------------------

# Flip the Script: Recognizing Your Superpower

Take a moment to reframe a thought you've had before—how can you turn it into a kind and encouraging one? For example, instead of thinking *"She's so much better at this than I am,"* try saying: *"I'm proud of how hard I'm trying."*

----------------------------------------------------------------------------------------

----------------------------------------------------------------------------------------

----------------------------------------------------------------------------------------

# Power Pose + Affirmation

**Let's try it again, stand tall, take a deep breath, and say to yourself: "Being myself is my superpower." Because it is! No one else has your exact mix of talents, dreams, and experiences. The world needs *you*, just as you are.**

Reflection: How does it feel to celebrate *yourself* instead of comparing yourself? Keep reminding yourself: "No one is me, and that is my superpower."

**Reminder: You deserve the same kindness you give to others. Instead of comparing yourself to someone else, try seeing yourself through the eyes of a friend—someone who loves and believes in you. Everyone has strengths and struggles, even if they don't show them. You are growing, learning, and doing your best, and that's more than enough. Be gentle with yourself—your journey is yours, and that's pretty special.**

YOU ARE
NEVER
BEHIND.
YOU ARE
EXACTLY
WHERE YOU
ARE MEANT
TO BE.

# *How Do You* SHINE?

**Strengths**: Identify your unique strengths and qualities. What makes you shine?

**Hopes**: Reflect on your aspirations and goals. What are you striving toward?

**Inspiration**: What inspires you and keeps you motivated? Who are your role models?

**Needs**: Recognize what you need to thrive—whether it's support, rest, or new opportunities.

**Empowerment**: Take action to step into your power. What's one thing you can do today to embrace your shine?

## S – Strengths

**Prompt:** What are your unique strengths, qualities, and talents? Think about what you're really good at, whether it's sports, creativity, kindness, or something else.

**Reflect:** Write down at least three strengths that make you proud of yourself. How do these strengths help you in your everyday life or in your goals?

*Examples:* I'm a good listener and always make people feel heard. I'm strong and can push myself through challenges.

## H – Hopes

**Prompt:** What are your biggest dreams and aspirations? What do you hope for yourself?

**Reflect:** Write down one or two big dreams you have for your future. These could be related to school, sports, personal growth—anything! How do you envision yourself achieving them?

*Examples:* I hope to become a more confident speaker and share my thoughts with others. OR I hope to run a marathon and feel strong while doing it.

# I – Inspiration

**Prompt:** Who or what inspires you? It could be a person, a book, a song—anything!

**Reflect:** Who is your biggest role model, and what qualities do they have that you admire? What inspires you to keep going, especially when things get tough?

*Examples:* My mom inspires me because she works hard and never gives up, no matter the challenge. The story of Malala Yousafzai inspires me to stand up for what I believe in.


# N – Needs

**Prompt:** What do you need to feel your best? This could be physical, emotional, or social needs.

**Reflect:** Think about what helps you feel supported and at ease. Are there things you need to ask for more of, like rest, encouragement, or a break from social media?

*Examples:* I need time to relax and recharge after a busy week. I need to ask for more help from my friends when I feel stressed.


# E – Empowerment

**Prompt:** How can you take action to step into your power and shine? What is one thing you can do today to feel more empowered?

**Reflect:** Write down one action that can help you feel stronger, more confident, or more aligned with your goals. It could be something small, like speaking up in a class or taking a new fitness class, or something bigger like setting a boundary with someone.

*Examples:* I will speak up in class today and share my thoughts, even if I feel nervous. I will remind myself of my strengths every morning to start my day with confidence.


**Reflection: Once you've filled out the SHINE exercise, take a moment to reflect on what you've written. How does it feel to recognize your strengths and think about what empowers you? Use the next page to write or draw out what makes you SHINE and put it somewhere you'll see it often (like your mirror, locker, or bedroom wall) as a reminder of your power!**

**This is how I SHINE:**

my
STRENGTH

my HOPE

my
INSPIRATION

my NEEDS

my
EMPOWERMENT

# Gratitude Cards

Take some time to reflect on things in your life that you are currently grateful for—they can be big or small! Write, draw or create a collage to illustrate a few of the top things that come to mind, from a delicious iced matcha latte to snuggles with your dog.

# Gratitude Cards

If you want to make sure you remember things you're grateful for, cut these cards up and stick them in places where you'll stumble across like, like in your wallet or hidden in your phone case!

# BEING YOURSELF IS THE BRAVEST THING YOU'LL EVER DO.

# *The Butterfly Effect:*
# Compassion Towards Others

Compassion isn't just about big gestures—it's about the small things we do every day to show kindness and care. These small acts have the power to create a ripple effect, like the butterfly effect, where one small action can lead to much bigger changes in someone's day—and maybe even their life.

Think about it: When you show compassion, you never really know how far it might go. Maybe that smile you gave someone today made them feel seen. Maybe the compliment you gave someone made them feel more confident. One small act of kindness can spark a chain reaction that spreads even further than you could imagine, creating a kinder, more connected world.

**Here are some ways to practice compassion in everyday life:**
- Helping a friend who's feeling overwhelmed – Sometimes, just being there to listen or offer a hand can make all the difference.
-  Including someone in a conversation or activity – You never know who's feeling left out, but your inclusion might make them feel like they belong.
- Giving a genuine compliment – Words can lift someone's spirits and remind them of their value.
- Leaving a kind note for someone – A little surprise kindness can brighten someone's day.
- Listening when someone needs to talk – Sometimes, just being a good listener can show someone you care.
- Saying thank you to someone who helped you – Gratitude can create a positive loop of appreciation and goodwill.

**Reflect:**

Think about a time you've shown compassion to someone else. How did it feel in that moment? How do you think it impacted that person, even if you didn't see it right away? By practicing kindness, you're part of a bigger, more beautiful shift.

------------------------------------------------------------

------------------------------------------------------------

------------------------------------------------------------

------------------------------------------------------------

------------------------------------------------------------

------------------------------------------------------------

What are five small ways you can practice compassion towards others this week?

------------------------------------------------------------

------------------------------------------------------------

------------------------------------------------------------

------------------------------------------------------------

------------------------------------------------------------

------------------------------------------------------------

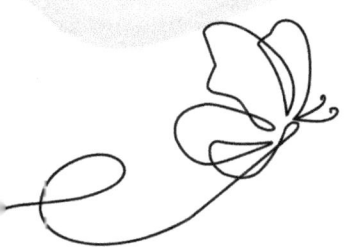

# YOU ARE
# WHAT YOU LOVE,
# WHAT YOU DREAM,
# AND HOW YOU MAKE
# OTHERS FEEL.

# A Letter to Me: *My Compassionate Self*

Writing a letter to yourself can feel silly at first, but it's a powerful way to practice self-compassion and to help yourself navigate hard moments. You can use this exercise anytime you need it, but take time now to practice writing a letter like this so you're ready when you need it next!

**Practice writing a compassionate letter to yourself:**
 - Imagine you have a best friend who always supports you: What would they say to you if you were feeling down or struggling with something?
 - Write yourself a letter using kind and encouraging words, just like a best friend would.
 - You can start with: "Dear [your name], I want you to know..." or "I see how hard you try, and I want to remind you..."

*Some other Prompts to Get You Started:*
### Acknowledgment & Appreciation:
- Dear body, I want to thank you for…
- One thing I appreciate about you is…
- I recognize that you help me every day by…

### Apology & Forgiveness:
- I now realize that when I said/did ___, it was unfair to you because…
- I'm sorry for the times I have…
- I forgive myself for…

### Commitment to Kindness & Respect:
- Moving forward, I will try to treat you with more kindness by…
- Instead of being critical, I will remind myself that…
- I promise to take care of you by…

### Reflection & Compassion:
- If I were speaking to a friend about their body, I would tell them…
- If my body could talk back to me, I think it would say…
- One way I can show my body compassion today is…

# *My Compassionate Self*

# *My* **MIRROR** *Contract*

I, _____, promise to treat myself with kindness every day.
I commit to:

**Speaking Kindly to Myself**
I will use gentle and encouraging words when I talk to myself, just like I would with a friend.

**Appreciating My Unique Qualities**
I will celebrate what makes me special, and remember that everyone is different in wonderful ways.

**Forgiving My Mistakes**
I understand that everyone makes mistakes. I will learn from them and not be too hard on myself.

**Taking Care of My Body and Mind**
I will rest when I need to, nourish my body to flourish, move my body in ways that feel good, and do things that make me happy.

**Asking for Help When I Need It**
I know it's okay to ask for support from family, friends, or teachers.

**Standing Up for Myself and Others**
I will be brave and speak up if I or someone else is not being treated kindly.

**Practicing Gratitude**
I will notice and appreciate the good things about myself and my life.

I promise to do my best to treat myself with kindness and respect every day.
When I forget, I will gently remind myself and try again.

Signed: _____

Date: _____

*You can print this out, decorate it, and sign it as a daily reminder of your commitment to self-kindness!*

# *References + Resources*

The worksheets and exercises in this workbook are evidence-informed and draw upon research across several key themes: body appreciation and functionality, self-compassion and mindfulness, positive psychology interventions, and social-psychological strategies.

Want to learn more or get a PDF version of this workbook to print? Visit **StrongGirlPublishing.com/beyond-the-mirror** or scan the QR code here to  access more printable worksheets, pump-up playlists + more!

ABOUT THE AUTHOR: Vanessa Coulbeck is a researcher focused on body image, self-compassion, and physical activity among girls. She has worked with national and international organizations to develop educational tools and evidence-informed strategies that promote body acceptance, self-compassion, and inclusive physical activity. Vanessa's work bridges academic, nonprofit, and innovation sectors, with a focus on real-world impact and well-being. She has presented her work at national and global conferences, including the World Health Organization's Physical Activity Congress, the European Congress of Sport, and has contributed to discussions and shared her work at the United Nations Headquarters. She continues to lead and advise on innovative projects that empower girls and women in movement spaces.

www.ingramcontent.com/pod-product-compliance
Lightning Source LLC
Chambersburg PA
CBHW041154120626
46547CB00020B/3205